CW00921196

Spectral Realms

No. 12 ‡ Winter 2020

Edited by S. T. Joshi

The spectral realms that thou canst see
With eyes veil'd from the world and me.

H. P. LOVECRAFT, "To a Dreamer"

SPECTRAL REALMS is published twice a year by Hippocampus Press,
P.O. Box 641, New York, NY 10156 (www.hippocampuspress.com).
Cover art by Albert Joseph Pénot, "La Femme Chauve-Souris" (c. 1890).
Cover design by Daniel V. Sauer, dansauerdesign.com
Hippocampus Press logo by Anastasia Damianakos.

ISBN 978-1-61498-289-0   ISSN 2333-4215

Contents

Poems

Acrostic Sonnet for Wilum Hopfrog Pugmire

David Barker

When evening shadows fall on Sesqua Vale
I wander down the violet-misted path,
Long seeking out the one whose singing hath
Lured many silver-eyed to leave the trail
In search of means to penetrate the veil
And pass into the Dreamlands, then Kadath,
My goal to halt his monstrous aftermath,
Perhaps to tempt the dog-faced boy to wail.

Unfortunately, none have seen him here.
Gates he once used, their rusted hinges creak;
Mold chokes the streams, their waters clogged with fear.
Indeed, he's not been spied on Selta's peak.
Returning night-gaunts circle without leer—
Else why no mouths if they had grief to speak?

Gray

M. F. Webb

'Tis quiet as the morning hours descend
And fog obscures the rain-abandoned street;
Heavy yet the sodden branches bend
With tumbling drops, as soft as padded feet.

Faintly now the sullen darkness lifts,
A gentle premonition of the day.
From out the shadows, measured colors sift
The daisies and nasturtiums ease from gray.

And here, a shadow seems to have a place
Upon a cushion lately occupied;
It turns and moves with newly founded grace
Beside the rose where late it would abide.

Then raises up and softly passes by
A brush of whisker, glint of golden eye.

Pilgrim in the Mist

Wade German

Through hills and valleys, quiet fields,
The mist is thick and never yields.
A path before me lies obscure;
Dimly discerned, it leads the way
In realms where men and cities were.

Beyond the twilight and the dawn,
The path winds ever on and on.
En route are temples I must tend,
Amid the mist that whispers, *"Stay,*
The gods are dead; thy quest must end."

But ever onward . . . I would sleep,
Forsake a while the vow I keep,
Wearing the fetters of a faith
That conquers in this corpse decay,
Continuing through weird mist, a wraith.

Proem to the Fortress Unvanquishable

Thomas Tyrrell

Dunsany, Irish peer of dreams,
Your fancies, fineries, and themes
Suffused my deeply dreaming nights
With all the terrors and delights
Of oozy Yann and Babbulkund
And realms of dream that lie beyond
The functional and drably grey
Cities inhabited by day.
When work was a lacklustre chore
And sleep a torture to endure
For fitful fevers plagued my rest,
And life itself seemed robbed of zest,
One visionary glimpse of those
Dreamlands you shadowed out in prose
Came like a draught of cool sweet wine,
Soothing those anguished thoughts of mine,
Lifting my nightmare-ridden curse.
So I retold in ballad verse
How Leothric, with force and wile,
Battled the metal crocodile,
How Sacnoth from the corpse was wrought
Stronger than steel, swifter than thought,

How evil things loathed and abhorred
That hero with his magic sword,
How, vanquished with one broken spell,
The nightmare's fearful castle fell,
That those whose nights are plagued with pain
Might read, and rest, and dream again.

Ode to the Great God Pan

Carl E. Reed

When frolicking fingers mothlike flit
    upon priapic purple
to flick & tease like o'er-pollen'd bees
    the stamen of bewitching myrtle

then all is well; all will be well
    for lusting summer boys
envisioning centaur, satyr, & faun
    hard masters of their joys

Ghebulax

Maxwell I. Gold

Under a starry cyber-web filled with bytes of malice, I felt the impending weight of a cold, faceless evil, preparing to swallow what remained of my unfortunate spirit. In the corporeal sadness of this lonely state, I wandered under oppressive neon stars whose sinister fluorescence chirped in my ears. Their sounds taunted my senses, like an unholy music with a melody so dark and hypnotic that it led me to traipse about the streets of the city I once called my home.

Soulless and empty, my body withered under the grim economic schizophrenia that had strangled the world in a form most familiar to me. As the concrete transformed to plastic, my eyes strained against the waning chaos, where towering metallic skeletons moaned in the spectral glow of the night. Their arthritic bodies creaked under the weight of oxidizing trusses as I walked beneath them. Like me, they were also subject to the dark arithmetic of a faceless creature who calculated their doom with cold symbols and black logic spoken in tones so foul. It was the sound of a deep viral strangulation, echoing the lamentations of a thousand dead races whose last hopes passed into silence, mere numbers in the dark. I watched as the daytime stars soon twitched and spiraled with a blasphemous mania, falling against the blue horizons tapering off toward a purple night, preparing to devour what was left of them.

At the bottom of the world, I sat pondering when death might bring me its sweet release. Deep in the alleyways of a defiled city of plastic and dust, that monstrous obscenity had confined me to a reality built in the image of its algebraic gruesomeness. Under a starry cyber-web filled with bytes of malice, I felt the impending weight of a cold, faceless evil, preparing to swallow what remained of my unfortunate spirit.

The Crimson Knight

Scott J. Couturier

A knight in crimson armor stands
upon a crimson shore:
waves break at her iron-beaked feet,
swells of godly gore.
She had come to taste of this red sea
& thus immortal become:
Yet now, Death seems more a friend
than foe to begrudge a sum.
She has come to pity the Gods for their
excesses & their might—
She has seen the vales of endless wrack,
the weals of Promethean night.
She has slain a thousand, thousand men,
enfeebled countless more,
all to reach these ichor-imbued sands,
this rank & crimson shore.
She stares, and is appalled by crawling
things that flop & moan:
her gorge rises as the seaside froths
with semi-sentient foam.
Her sword, chipped & stained to jet
by blood of lover, friend, & foe
now is driven deep into her heart—

a barb of bitterest woe.
Out amid the erubescent waves
Titans up-stir, wail & cry:
That she should come so far to attain
what all inherit—that is, to die.

Haematophagy

Ashley Dioses

Deep scarlet hearts were pressed upon pale skin
By Nadia's soft and satin bloodstained lips.
She drank from lovers' steaming streams in sips
And purred against the cooling forms of twins.
Amid their orgic play she wore a grin;
She traced their veins with reddened fingertips
And pricked their tender skin while hip to hip.
Their necks were last, a treat of sweetest sin.

The Countess lay among her loves, and yet
They quickly grew too boring, cold and dead.
In truth no one could be her deathless pet.
The bodies were no use to her once bled,
So to a Sorceress she gave away
The twins for her to use in her own way.

Not All of Them Are Ghosts

Darrell Schweitzer

Not all the voices you hear in the night
are necessarily ghosts.

The long, mournful howling
that goes "o—o—o" without many message
might be an amorous owl, but more likely
it's the wind blowing over a pipe.

The voice that says exactly what you said
in perfect agreement, even as it fades,
is an echo.

The harping, hectoring, jabbering
that criticizes every detail of your life
and screams for you to do outrageous things
is inside your head.
You're having a psychotic break.

But the voices that strain to be heard
like someone buried alive, clawing for air and light,
the ones that ask you only to weep
as they plead for you to tell their stories,
recall their faces, remember their loves and sorrows,
the ones that only under the most extraordinary circumstances
demand revenge,

those might be ghosts.

Poe, on the Morning After

Don Webb

After the visits of my vampire lover
After the bites and the bruises
From my harsh cruel muses
After the thousandth time of wondering if she **really** is a vampire
My world becomes a shaky nauseating kaleidoscope
Now fever dream, now chilly weakness,
Now summer, now winter,
Now flowers, now ash.
Ah, I remember it was in the bleak December
And I, a dying ember, wrought my ghost upon the floor;
And as I fade into that final ashy dream I tell myself
The remedy for my pain
Is the pain itself.

Homage to *Creepy*

Manuel Pérez-Campos

Never in a million bats will you find
in these worm-cropped black-and-white panoramas
stretched like a rotten bridge across a two-
page splash nightmares gorier than these
newly risen out of fogged swamp muck to
loosen the hold of daytime on your mind.
Here be tales gleefully unapproved by
the Comics Code from the nightlong country:
Here be subtle doubles of yourself tendered
by a cloaked sleazy-faced MC with only change
of hairstyle or modish costume to make you strange
and limn more vividly what seems absurd:
a speech balloon in which you exchange
mature content for an *aarrgh* or *ai-eee*
because a comet's tail has turned you beastly.

Xipe Totec

Deborah L. Davitt

They flayed me alive,
draped my skin
over a statue of the god,
so that the red flesh clung
to the stone—

the priests didn't know
that he kept me alive,
even as they took my skin
from him to wear
as vestments in the fields.

As they prayed
for the corn to grow,
they didn't know
that I followed them,
leaving red footprints
in the black earth;

didn't know
that my teeth bared white
against the ragged,
bleeding hole
that was my mouth;

didn't know
that it was their flesh,
their blood,
their sacrifice,
that would renew the earth—

but I did,
because the god walked with me
and I was him
and he was me—
one set of red footprints
in the black earth.

Necronomicon

Josh Maybrook

Bound in chains
It gathers mold,
Harboring secrets
Aeons old.

What strange truths
Would be revealed
If its clasps of iron
Were unsealed?

And what horrors
Would it evoke
If its cryptic text
One rashly spoke?

Wretched Raft

Kieran Dacey Boylan

Troves of rotting treasures
Marked the highest morning tide
Where the ocean's foaming tongue
Left its print upon the land.
I trifled with the sea wrack
That was scrawled upon the sand
When a seaborne scent came wafting;
Onward sailing to the shore.

Pale, aghast, I stood in awe
To curse the wretched thing I saw.

Yet counting footprints from the scene
The vision haunts me all the more;
Forever sailing to the fore
Upon the winds of sordid thoughts,
Where my mind is ever stained,
Though one question there remains—
How a body, once alive,
Could be so full of eels.

Satanic Sonata

(On Hearing Eyvind Kang's "Universal")

Manuel Arenas

It is late in the year, on a pitchy night over the potter's field in a small
New England cemetery. The vault of heaven appears moonless, starless,
and smothering in its blackness, which hangs like a funereal mantle over
the unconsecrated grounds where lie, uneasily, the disconsolate shades
of the wicked and unwanted. Beyond the unmarked plots of the indigent
there is a rumbling tremor in the grounds as a fissure forms in the
unblest soil of the quarter reserved for criminals, suicides, and decedents
of questionable virtue or creeds. Gradually increasing in size, the rent
erupts into a sizeable crevasse, belching forth reeking clods of burning
sulfur and blue flames.

   Like smoke from snuffed-out candles, anguished souls rise in
phantasmal wisps; summoned from their cold carcasses, they wail in
unison a single woeful plaint before being snatched into the abyss.
Emerging from the pit are two hell-born sons, their seared hides bearing
a ruddy hue. The first, a long-shanked sinewy devil with a mannish head,
grins a toothy smile, his yellow eyes staring at the empty spaces between
the licks of flame as they lap at the perimeter of the pit. Perching on the
shoulders of a headstone of a burking resurrectionist whose infernal
punishment is to remain in his perpetually putrefying cadaver, the devil
scrapes and scratches a discordant air on a fiddle made of coffin wood,
and strung with the innards of a sinner. Like a leering grotesque, he
squats, stock-still, as his bow arm flails frenziedly at his sepulchral
instrument.

Across the chasm, facing the fiddler, is a stubby devilkin with bovine features and ossicone-like protuberances on his brow. In his chubby hands he holds a large curled horn hewn from the skull of a massive and unfamiliar creature. His languid eyelids half closed, his expression almost serene, he purses his lips, protrudes his bulbous paunch, and blows a dirgeful tone that rattles the remains of the abutting boneyard tenants. Mingling with the cloven-hoofed din is the pitter-patter of raindrops from a sudden cloudburst, sizzling as they dissipate on the parched rictus of the minikin hell-mouth providing a continuo accompaniment for the cacophonic recital.

But the downpour proves to be no match for the doomful gripe of unquenchable fire and shadow as it swirls from out of the brimstone pit to grasp at the ethereal quarry within its forbidding clutches, and the diabolical duo's tuneful profanity whirls across the tenebrous welkin, even unto the main kirkyard, to lacerate the peaceful slumbers of the goodly dead.

Time's Vulture

Leigh Blackmore

Unvanquishable Time doth swoop and sweep
To bring its presence, cause a growing gloom.
From birth to death we can but lie so deep
Within its grip of creeping, clutching doom.

Time's Vulture is a deadly bird that roams
Upon the Earth where empires fall and rise,
And on the sea where emerald ocean foams,
And in the sullen cloud-towers of the skies.

Nocturnal moths lie sleeping in the rust.
The Vulture's fatal, rending, red-mouthed kiss,
Makes amethystine diamonds rot to dust
And planets cease to roll in the abyss.

The full moon wanes, effaced by cruel claws
And suns of ages golden fade away;
The Vulture sinks its talons, snaps its jaws
Upon the worlds where sorrow now holds sway.

Time's Vulture hangs aloft o'er all our lives,
Its carrion wings cast shadows on the sands.
Mortality, despotic, sink its knives
Into our hearts with ultimate demands.

The hovering oblivion blights our nights
When dark thoughts prey inside our dreaming heads.
And skulls of kings bear witness to last rites
That haunted them when *they* lay in their beds.

Urban Renewal

Mike Allen

the plagues seeped through the city's cracks,
immunizations reviled and denied, immunity lost

windows swelling into sores, doors
sealed open, paralyzed jaws

skyscrapers shedding mold-black chunks,
red rot unveiled beneath

roads puckered with pox,
subways blocked by venous polyps

gutters flooded with leaking lymph
between suppurating façades

the pestilence of cars and commerce
still struggling upstream

to seek out the last oases of health,
feed until depletion and breed in the remains

Graveside Ghost

Mary Krawczak Wilson

He appeared in the shadow
Of the great old oak,
Singed in ash and smoke
From a fire lit long ago.

She visits cemeteries
Searching for headstones
Of those so alone
Now laid beneath graying trees.

He ventured from his gate post
To the wraith so pure,
Intending to lure
Her to his dark world of ghosts.

She began to walk away,
But his fetid breath
Lulled her to near death
Before he led her astray.

No One Is Safe

Benjamin Blake

It creeps through the weeds
Like a hungry house cat
Seeking the heart
That pumps warm blood
Through plump, ripened veins.

Shadows like snakes
Coil around trellis
Slither and climb through rose thorn
Toward an open window.

She sits, brushing golden hair
In the mirror's polished glass,
Night-slip leaving little to the imagination;
Something dark slides over the sill
And drops silent to the bedroom floor.

Something's wrong—
A feeling along the inner thigh
Like little pinpricks of heat,
There and then gone.
She pauses, hairbrush in hand,
But those gilded strands
Continue to stir

*   *   *

Eyes wide
Mouth agape.
She scrabbles at her throat with painted nails
As it enters
And proceeds to feed
From the inside out.

Minoan Messages

Frank Coffman

Where Thera lay, proud Minoan colony,
The island town of Santorini lies
In terraces of stark white 'gainst the skies,
Rising in beauty above the azure sea.

Near four millennia later, most scholars think
This place gave birth to Plato's wondrous story
Of Great Atlantis and its fabled glory
And how that glory 'neath the sea did sink.

And they were prosperous, wonderfully advanced—
Long, long ago before the Earth rebelled
And from its angry bowels foul Death expelled—
They throve and were happy ere disaster chanced.

They were proud citizens of a marvelous nation.
Miles to the south, King Minos' land—now Crete—
Held sway with scion Thera. A great fleet
Ruled trade all through that early civilization.

But came a day of wonder and stark terror,
A day of fire and tremors, hot steam and death—
When flesh was melted or the ash-stopped breath
Left none alive who once had reveled there.

It's likely there was some warning, and a fleet
Set sail to the south, the Theran folk to save—
Only to sink when the great tsunami wave
Swept o'er them and moved on to ruin Crete.

Then Mycenæans and others from mainland Greece—
As archaeo-historical records show—
Soon claimed the islands, laid the Minoans low
Through years of war, until they reigned in peace.

But such is the persistency of humankind
That, after centuries, things buried in long death
Will, once again, spring forth—as if new breath
Revived the dead and gone, things lost to mind.

And Knossos' labyrinthine ways were found,
With frescoes wondrous and a stone-hewn throne!
In long-dead Thera—what no one had known—
Advanced Akrotiri struggled from the ground!

And, just as Keats had noted about the urn,
Art has its ways of keeping things alive,
And things once lost can be found, bloom, and thrive—
The artists' fires of passion once more burn.

Just so, in Knossos and Thera there are souls—
Not only of the spirit but material,
Works at once substantial and æthereal—
Immortal: chief of every Artist's goals.

Bare-breasted beauties with flagons of fine wine
Or harvesting saffron from the crocus flower—
They still enthrall the eye with a mystic power,
Although their models long in dust recline.

In one, a fresco of a strange pastime,
A lad leaps over a bull—he's frozen there,
Never to find the earth from the blue-paint air.
But nowise dead. The lad has leapt past Time.

Madhouse Getaway

Manuel Pérez-Campos

A sybil-crone of laconic deviltry
is she in state-issued tunic of grey
and knee-length hair begirt by spate of homegrown
weeds. As unremarkable as any
of us is she, and yet we have made altars to
her. She is the queen of passing through,
for she can project, although bedstead-strapped,
through chills from mumbled incantation,
numbnesses to us who heed that we may
suffer this premature brownstone sepulchre
not again: for when glowing creepers flare
out of her mouth and topple us enlooped
downstairs as a keen, blossom-rich mêlée,
our guts puffed or ruptured from white worm rapture,
some of us shall shred, some branch out past moan
as we, supine, ooze and claw across fought corridors
and slither out through sills and gaping doors.

Planet Fetish

Chad Hensley

From far up in the atmosphere
I look down through the thick glass,
Pasty face pressed against the clear, chilled pane,
The first drops of drool beginning to fall from wet lips.
Mesmerized by the great expanse of lush beauty beneath me,
Temples pounding with blood; lust-hunger of impotent aeons
An infernal machine in my veins.

As if on cue:
Dark fissures spread in vast directions
Like a sea of spider webs
Shredding the perfect smoothness of parted thighs.
Faster than my eyes can follow,
Deep lacerations open and close
Like fevered mouths sucking at moist secret places.
Tidal waves of flame swollen with excitement
Spray cherry-orange magma over buildings, cities, continents,
Exposing her sex,
Sizzling and radioactive.
A rapid burst of thermonuclear kisses
Cauterizes the succulent flesh in a second as pure as pornography,
Microscopic computer cells pumping
Manufactured endorphins into spasming brain tissue.

Soon I am higher than the clouds,
Blotting out the incinerating plains beneath me.

I can only climb higher,
Locked into the billowing white afterglow of time-lapsed orgasm.
Tiny whorls of smoldering soot swirl skyward like burst blood vessels,
The spent seed of past intercourse spilling into the burning horizon,
Scent of sex and death tainting the shriveled atmosphere
Centuries after I am gone.

Jack in Xanadu

Adam Bolivar

Jack wandered far, far to the east,
Where few had gone, not man or beast,
To win some gold, a tale at least,
Which he might tell at some king's feast.

And there he found it: Xanadu.
    A ruin now it lay,
Whose former shape he could construe
    Neath æons of decay.

It was a place where dreamers met
    To hear a phantom lyre,
To drink a drug and to forget
    The ache of their desire.

Jack thought he glimpsed a scarlet ghost
    Who strummed a black guitar,
The damsel who had loved him most;
    He heard her from afar.

"I sang for thee, O golden hair,
    My lovely blue-eyed Jack;
There never lived a man as fair,
    But I am dead, alack!"

Upon the ground Jack found a vial,
    Unstoppered it to drink,
To let the opium beguile
    And into dreams to sink.

Dream is a land close by to death,
    Where Jack his lover found;
Tantivy was his shibboleth
    And made his horn resound.

They shared a single night these two,
    A night of scarlet sin,
Until they had to bid adieu
    To that romantic inn.

In Xanadu Jack then awoke
    Upon a bed of stone,
And shivering, dew-drenched his cloak,
    Once more he was alone.

Genesis

Holly Day

the tiny seeds drift with sand
shift with the tilting wings
like boats on the ocean
waiting for rain.

what forgotten flowers might bloom
from seeds set free in the desert
blown from ancient windowboxes
escaping from damaged cargo, perhaps

the gardens of Babylon
have lain dormant for millennia, riding the shifting crests
of sand dunes
waiting for rain.

I Want to Taste October

Ross Balcom

I want to taste October.

I want to lick its headstones,
thrust my tongue into the mouths of ghouls.

I want to taste October.

I want to blacken my tongue on burning leaves,
slice it on razor blades concealed in apples.

I want to taste October.

I want to taste my blood running free,
a red river with no boatman.

I want to taste October.

I want to taste death on death on death,
corpses piled higher and higher.

I want to taste October,

want to taste the end of all things,
my soul impaled on Oblivion's spire.

A Tasty Treat

Adele Gardner

The kitchen is the best room in the house.
Not just for warmth, but precious memories—
Two grandmas baking treats and brewing spells,
My crafty decorations on the walls—
My heroes—Nimue and Morgan Faye,
And wise Italian cats who duel and scrap
And come to life at night to prowl my halls
And keep me safe from demons in the walls.
Why not live for gingerbread? I crave
The comfort of a batch already made
And waiting in the freezer for my touch
To bring a horse, boy, star, or Santa Claus
To life within my kiln with magic stuff
You can't get at the store. The children come,
As children always do, drawn by the smell,
The magic dancing ready in their eyes.
I'll bake them up a magical surprise.
The taste will bring your childhood flooding back;
It's toasty warm upon my baking rack.

Beyond the Fields

Andrew J. Wilson

What lies in wait for you and me
    Beyond the fields we know we know?
There only is one way to see
What lies in wait for you and me
Through the gates of the silver key:
    Into the Dreamlands we must go . . .
What lies in wait for you and me?
    Beyond the fields, we know, we know!

To the memory of Dunsany and Lovecraft

The Tears of Cerberus

Wade German

In the histories of the poets, there is much related concerning the watchdog of Hades, whose eternal task it was to prevent the souls of the dead from fleeing the gates of hell; but in all those annals, there is no mention that he perpetually wept.

The tears that trailed from his sextuple eyes flowed to form black crusts, like risen veins, upon his cheeks. Born with the evil intelligence of the primordial chthonic class, but also with an instinctual love of man, his three brains came to loathe the duty imposed on him by his god and master, and his melancholy howls haunted the borderlands of hell.

The mixture of tears and slobber that stained his muzzle mingled with ectoplasm that continually dripped from his jaws (for while conflicted, he was devout in devouring the fleeing ghosts of the damned).

From those drops sprang beautiful petals that became the symbol of love equaled with lethality: the lugubrious blue emblem of all that is loathed.

A Witch in the House

Oliver Smith

They prized away
the grey-as-a-widow doorstep,
the limestone worn
by near a half-millennium
of mud-crusted boots,
bare-feet creeping,
slippers' soft-steps
in the midnight mist.
Sealed with a sign

—in a old green bottle:
the witches' bones—
cremated ash from her fingers,
toes, spine, and skull-cap
buried under home-stone
to keep evil from the threshold.
We unstopped the house-stone,
unstopped the hearth,
unstopped her heart:

she scraped inside:
the fruit of a withered vine.
She knocked and tapped:
an aged vintage.
From the lip she floated
in an unseen wind;

eyes like blue-lightning
burning in an unseen, unholy
unloved wind

that upended chairs and tables,
candles, teapots, saucepans.
Her fingers all afire
from the sky she plucked
the crescent moon;
from the still pool she plucked
the crescent moon;
from her darkened mirror
she plucked the crescent moon.

She took a hundred forms:
the owl that flies,
the silhouetted bat
melancholia-black against the stars . . .
hanging in the sky,
the moth on dusty silent wings;
she is the wind that whispers;
whispers with dead lips
in the void.

Now the rusted bolt
is shot and the door barred

with a strong oak beam,
but with no threshold guard
what use dread prayers
declaimed on bended knee?
Grown in darkness, grown in hell and hate,
Grown again a witch is free
and awaits us in the night.

The Psychopomp

Cecelia Hopkins-Drewer

There she sits, rocking on her back porch,
A crazy old lady nodding her head;
Halloween Eve, the moon her torch:
They say that cats can see the dead.

Feline on her lap, her only company;
She nods off to sleep, but wakes in fright,
Because the air is chilling suddenly.
Strange the cold change in the bright night.

The cat wakes too, and it hisses.
"What do you see, Cuddles—
Something the old eye misses?"

My eyes are open, I see a shadow
Rise from my mistress, lose its features;
Across the garden, over the meadow,
Lost in the shouts of trick and treaters.

Morning brings an ambulance van white.
They enter the yard through the side gate,
Lay my owner on a stretcher held tight,
Carrying the body way while I wait.

The cat was left behind, and it hissed.
"What did you see, Cuddles—
Something the old eye missed?"

The Plague Queen's Song

Nicole Cushing

I.

The shattered king on cursèd throne
wears black boils on his face.
The shattered king has always known
you cringe at his embrace.

You grasp at glamour, gowns and gold
but shun the liege who grants them.
You run from that damned king—so old!—
and steal a king's ransom.

He whimper-wails for you to come
to him as death draws nigh.
You hide and seek a way to numb
the guilt of being sly.

Alone, the king must die.

II.

The shattered king's thrown on a pyre,
no crypt, no grave, no priest.
For he's dead too, just like your sire,
and every prayer has ceased.

So off you go to find a new
King or Prince or Duke,

but as you traipse across the dew
skulls scream at you, "Beware!"

For Death has nearly conquered all,
upon pale hearts He dines.
You're all alone and now a thrall
to prophecies and signs.

The Red Star dims and shines.

III.

Therefore your nerves begin to twist
and coil and fray and break.
You feel a cold grasp on your wrist
but see no hand to take.

The king's voice echoes out from Hell,
"Come down and hole me, dear!"
And all the world's a prison cell
ran by the warden, Fear.

You put mud in your ears, despise
the onslaught of the sound.
But soon he's there before your eyes.
Once lost, now you've been found.

He's tracked you like a hound.

IV.

He's now a fiend with crimson claws
and skin the shade of rust.
He shrieks his findings of your flaws.
He speaks of betrayed trust.

You push away his ghastly head;
it crumbles in your hand,
turned back to ash. The breeze is fed,
with crushed bones and gray sand.

And so you think the danger's o'er,
And grateful hymns are sung.
But then you feel the ashes pour
upon your chanting tongue.

And soon they fill a lung.

V.

The shattered king died all alone
and then was left to burn.
So now for that you must atone:
You'll be his human urn.

Constancy you shall learn.

I'll Return in Late October

K. A. Opperman

I'll return in late October,
When my grave is flecked with leaves,
And my name has nearly vanished
Where the ivy slowly weaves.

I'll return in late October,
When a crimson sunbeam falls
On a tomb that time has banished,
Where a somber raven calls.

I'll return in late October,
When a harvest gift is left
By a poet ghosts have guided
To my grave, forlorn, bereft.

I'll return in late October,
Like a phantom in your dreams,
When the witch has moon-ward glided,
And the jack-o'-lantern gleams.

The Philosophy & Aesthetics of Horror

Carl E. Reed

Horror should be beautiful, quoth the corpse;
herewith didactic verse bereft of chorus:
pumpkin-orange moon in jet-black sky,
parchment & palimpsest brown & dry,

brittle-crackle warding words & spells,
priapic goatish demons out of hell,
crimson-purple spatter o'er stone
clanking iron chains—thin moan & groan:

dungeon prisoner writhing in the dark,
glint of steel & reddish hissing spark,
top-hatted butcher wreathed in mist & fog,
fleshless victims rising from the bog.

The beauty of all horror sums to this:
eternity is bottomless abyss.
Book & bell & candle, flute & horn
prove powerless 'gainst beetle, moth, & worm.

Man is born to preen & strut & die—
he ponders, reproduces, laughs & cries;
ever seeking answer to the *why?*
till existential angst turn nihilist sigh.

Black Wings Return

Michael D. Miller

Have you ridden upon the raven's wings
That flap from vortices and fling
Far outside windows of distant places?
Along nebulaic forms adrift starry-eyed faces
To this infinitesimal speck return
Below the dome of tiny burning suns.
Every emperor entombed along the Appian Way
Did see me before this night,
And under tall silent cathedral spires
Redemptive priests and peasants once lined in pews
Did see me before this night and spake
Across the scars of time where concrete streets
Of vast electric cities folk mingle in delight.
Their temples cry with thoughts and prayers,
Their borders bleed with forsaken children,
And their marketplaces on this of all nights—
A throng of floating blue screens,
A multitude obscene—further my dark descent.
I am the flapping black thing
Drave my claws feathers out of heaven,
Ebony beak pecking out the eyes of those
Who tremble at the salient stars of oblivion
Where once upon a poet upon a windowsill

I cawed nevermore;
And now upon the world at all your windows
I tap forevermore
To ride upon my raven being
That flaps from vortices and sings of
Wondrous windows on distant places
Where black wings return and stardust traces.

Slow the Night Grows Darker

David Sammons

Sunset, earthquake, coastlines heave;
A city is revealed.
The place they said did not exist
Is suddenly made real.

Black seaweed clings to dome and spire,
Dripping in the gloom,
The silhouetted monuments
No longer are entombed.

Heavy fall the briny drops
From rooftops to the streets,
Drowning out strange noises
With their ceaseless drumming beat:

The scratching at the rotten wood
Of crypts and ancient doors,
A voice of rasping sibilance
That should not be ignored.

The city was the dwelling place
Of fiends down in the deep,
Which hunt the boats of fishermen
And haunt them in their sleep.

The evening sky is darkening,
The black walls hide the sun,

The shadows they are lengthening
And nightfall has begun.

In endless streets we lose our way
And fear that we are followed;
By moonlight we try to escape
This maze the ocean swallowed.

And surely we are fewer now,
As slow the night grows darker.
We navigate our way by sound,
The restless surf our marker.

Through winding shadow-haunted lanes
Too late the shore we've found!
As from the waves the horrors come,
Enslavers of the drowned.

Silent figures stand before us,
Silhouetted by the moon,
Their glassy eyes, their thick webbed claws
Point the way toward our doom.

A sailboat waits, the end is near,
The boatman gaunt and faceless
Whispers lessons of the tide;
We'll drown, but death won't save us.

The Wild Hunt

Chelsea Arrington

When the moon is foul and red with blood
And the birds no longer sing;
When the cows all freeze and trees don't bud
And the hoar of winter stings:

'Tis the time when Gwyn ap Nudd will ride
And he blows his horn of doom.
With his deathly hounds of Hell beside
They give chase to souls in gloom.

To the cradle he will calmly creep
And then sing a lullaby
To your baby girl in deepest sleep
Who'll then flicker, extinguish, and die.

He'll take Granny, Thatcher, Brewster, Hugh
(He was drinking in the fens).
He'll take Ma and me and even you.
He'll take everyone: rivals and friends.

For the thief of souls is Gwyn the White.
He has neither foe nor friend.
To him nothing's sad, he's not contrite,
Yet is father to all in the end.

Lines Written in a Providence Churchyard

David Barker

Here Pugmire scribed a verse, as did Lovecraft.
On yonder stone they sat and dreamed of Poe,
Perchance to glimpse his specter in this yard;
Fair Sarah Whitman nearby lived and laughed,
Remembering their romance brought forth woe.
Oh, weep for all in life that is so hard—
Gone are the ones we loved, they've fled this world,
Pale ghosts like leaves a chilling wind once swirled.

Unless their spirits linger 'neath the stones,
Grow old as fragile flesh falls in decay.
May St. John's Churchyard always harbor souls,
Interred or drawn to dwell among the bones.
Reviving shade of Edgar from the clay,
Embracing Howard, Wilum, and the ghouls.

The God of the Winds

Christina Sng

Beneath the heavens

When the night is still,
The god of the winds
Sends its arms down,

Lifts a house from a town
And sends it into
A spinning maelstrom,

Suspending it in the air,
A marionette without strings,
A puppet master in the sky,

Till it tires
Of this parlor trick
And lets everything fly,

Dropping the house
Fifty stories
Onto the ground,

A family strewn
All over the town,
Discarded dolls,

Broken and torn,
Casualties of the whims
Of the callous gods.

Singularity

Curtis M. Lawson

What things may be in that place which eats light?
What nightmares there dwell feasting upon time?
Ancient, dead gods of inverse paradigm?
Heavenly vistas or plains of Hell's blight?

Do dreams dance within that dense ever-night?
Is it pure nothing, empty and sublime,
Too perfect to capture in verse or rhyme,
Or is it chaos, complete and outright?

Do dark tendrils reach, seeking to benight,
Or does wisdom hide in its dense space-time—
Secrets of an entity first and prime?
A thing too perfect to see with plain sight?

What wonders swim in that cosmic, black sea?
What sirens sing to us with gravity?

Dream Hackers

Maxwell I. Gold

There they sat in dirty yellow hoodies, with eyes shrouded behind silver screens that were once the membranes of a person who knew better. Our eyes had become theirs, covered in glass, tapped and swiped along by the hungering grip of these things congealed in mountainous webs concocted of tweets, snaps, and replicated dreams. They were the nightmarers who wandered between the green pillars of a world offline while cyber things had fused themselves against their bodies, in a new form of symbiosis.

Despite the warnings we faced, the fears we felt, many of us ignored them. We dismissed them as outliers and pariahs, who existed simply as a waste, feeding off the margins of every vital byte, scrumming every ounce of our precious existence. Gnawing at the veritable edges of our cities, they left us vulnerable to the Cyber Gods, whose very vengeance we had invoked, and the dream hackers became their harbingers. Coming as they did with a thirst for the dreams that floated on oceans of computerized fantasies and infinite realities, there was nothing we could do to stop them. From protocols written with a logic so grim, to hideous Dreamwares installed on our neurons, acting as the servers to which they could sniff, phish, and suck us dry.

The last of the great cities was helplessly brought to its knees by the mere tap of a key, stroked gently with the touch of a finger; while under the hoods of dead eyes, their faces contorted with images pixelated in an awful twitch. The hackers had broken through the wall, and there was nothing they could do to stop them, there was nothing they could do to stop me. There I sat in my yellow hoodie, with eyes shrouded behind silver screens that were once the membranes of a person who knew better.

The Bedlam Philharmonic

Steven Withrow

Hank hates these concerts, finds them cloying,
But Lisa loves them, so here they are
On the mezzanine. Below, the star
Conductor preens. What's more annoying,
He turned down Red Sox tickets to make
His woman happy. For heaven's sake,

Let's wrap this up already, he thinks.
This Mahler song's ten hours long.
Just then he sees there's something wrong
With the lady playing cello. He blinks
And looks again. She sways in her chair,
With bony fingers, snaky hair.

The other players haven't changed,
Il Maestro hasn't missed a beat,
And Lisa's frozen to her seat
Oblivious to how deranged
The demon cellist now appears,
A fusion of his inmost fears.

Hank splutters, points, and nearly stands,
And Lisa briskly clears her throat
To show she's hanging on every note.
Woodwinds wheeze. The harpy's hands,
Outsized like crab claws, strangle strings,
And at her back, black angel's wings.

Mahler ends; crowd applauds;
Star conductor soaks it in;
Cellist gives a shark-toothed grin
As if to say that fiendish gods
Had favored theirs of all domains
With dismal and abysmal strains

Of noise, though Hank alone receives
The twisted signal. A standing ovation
Reverses the freakish transformation
In the cellist's frame. His brain believes
Such alteration's bunk. His eyes,
However, tell him otherwise.

At intermission, leaving the hall,
Lisa scowls, mistaking shock
For scorn on Hank's face, white as chalk.
"Next time stay home and watch baseball,"
She sneers and waits for Hank's dumb joke,
But none comes. It's like he's had a stroke

Or grand mal seizure. Choking, he stumbles
Against the wall and drops to the floor,
And Lisa's by his side and yelling for
Someone to call a doctor. He mumbles.
His fevered head is in her lap,
His round mouth closing like a trap.

The House (A Conduit)

Mack W. Mani

I.

I was born
in the lee of the world,
in the shadow of the house
a Summer Child
a commune-colony-cult
lost in the deepblue valley waves
of heady Appalachian heat.

We'd inherited the squatters' rights
from psychotronic professors
and horror movie thrill seekers,
fans of Shirley Jackson
and Richard Matheson
who came to see
"The Marianas Trench" of
haunted houses.

But where others fled and read and dare not tread
my mother and her fellow disciples
walked and worshipped,
ruined and reveled
in a world of their own devising.

I did not wear clothes regularly
until I was five,

I didn't know about money
until I was fifteen,
and monogamy remains
a mystery to me still.

I was raised on
campfire virtue, LSD,
and shuffled tarot wisdom,
every sign a symbol
and every symbol a sign
from God, the Gods, the Goddess—
it didn't seem matter then,
all were equal in
the womb of the house.

II.

Spirits came and went
at their leisure there,
most often in
the early morning blaze,
ghostly figures tracing
gnomic patterns in the wet
and quickening grass.

They never spoke
but seemed to me

of another mind,
dislodged of place and time,
their placid expressions
owed to another generation
of pain and revelry.

That vast estate,
with its paint-peeled walls
and gimcrack barracks,
were to me the world entire,
the crumbling porch
and sagging gambrel roof
a temple for the few
who thought they understood the place
and relayed its message
from on deep:

You are the wax
and I am the lantern;
enter here and be released,
enter me and be alive.

III.

One crisp and crackling summer morn
the council hanged my mother from the pines;
her crimes (if any) were not divulged,

but I will never forget her bare feet swinging,
black soles grazing the flowering tamarisk,
the wearied wrinkles of her face
gone purple in the bloat of death:

they woke me after
so that I could see,
so that I might bare witness
to her transformation.

They lowered her corpse
down the bridewell at dusk
and prayed she might
become one with house;
her only wish in life, they said,
to dissolve herself within its walls.

That night
they drank to her life
and gave her a new name
and gave me a new mother
and set about deciphering
the messages that she would leave
the signals she would send;
many members asked of me that night,
the rank of barrel whiskey
reeling on their tongues:

In what form will she return,
to walk the halls
of eternity?

IV.

A year or so later
men from the government came,
all handcuffs and hazmat suits,
caffeine pills and O_2 tanks
to protect them from
the influence of the grounds.

Children were pulled
from their wet nurse's chests
bodies exhumed from beneath the deck;
some of us tried to hold them off,
but we were no Waco, no Covenant,
and I when saw the armored vans
roll down the dusty drive
they seemed to me
greats beasts come from far,
come to kill the dream.

Then came the soft rooms
and therapy sites,
the deprogramming

and the myth of survival;
immersion confusion
lights and sounds and TV
all to drown out
the pull of the house
to strip it from our every mind.

But these many years later
I can feel it still,
tugging me gently back toward
the weedy fields
and overgrown greenhouse,
to the darkened halls
and dust-coat attic,
to the place where the dead walked
and the living sang
a strange and terrible song.

The Summer Children are gone
but the house remains,
I'm certain,
out there somewhere
half drowned in the autumn russet,
standing still a conduit for death.

I wonder if I'd find her there,
circling the dew wet grass,

or if she lies still
beneath the planks,
her heart as black
as the soles of her feet.

The Pack

Scott J. Couturier

Under light of a quickening moon
the Pack gathers in frenzy.
Musky scent: yellow eyes ablaze.
The pups nip & tumble, sharpening
incipient claws on trees.

Tonight, a raid. The taste of blood
peremptorily lingers on panting tongues.
Howls are sent up to the lunar orb:
wolf-hair bristles out from human
flesh as snouts elongate, sniff at dung.

To the wind! The wind! Following
rank mortal spoor: Skirt the churchyard,
snarl & stalk past frost-latticed panes.
The villagers hunker in the town
hall, arguing over their fate ill-starred.

The omens have been read: seen.
Gathering of pitchforks & torches,
old blades half-rusted in scabbard.
It has been long since war or famine
this remote woodland scorched.

Yet now: the howls rise from
all sides, orbs hot with hungry gleams
circling in twilight. A stench of wet
wolf-fur & offal accompanies the Pack:
The night fills with inhuman screams.

The townsfolk are foolish. The church
would have rendered some reprieve.
Instead, holed up in the village hall,
they wail & tear at clothing & hair—
some slay themselves as others grieve.

The Pack closes in: collective yearning
for the kill, for blood, rumbles their belly.
They cross the fence-line on hind legs
striding, talons bared & moonlight-bright—
inside, amassed prey quakes like jelly.

Prayers are offered as wolf-bodies
surge against frail clapboard walls.
Windows shatter: flames are brandished.
Children shriek & moan as the air
clouds with a pungent soot-&-canine pall.

The townsfolk are no match, no match
for primal fury recrudesced. Blindly
they stab with tine & blunted blade
as a flood of hairy bodies bursts into
the hall, borne on a reeking wind.

Wolfsbane burns! Wolfsbane burns!
The Pack shrieks as wreaths of it
fall on their shoulders: some are
garlanded, flesh & fur steaming acrid.
A bit of old lore the townsfolk found writ.

But: there is no stemming the tide
of supermundane sinew & jaws.
The men are slain, the women ripped.
Youths, herded tight in a passel,
are infected by clip of fang & claw.

Borne back into snow-clad wilderness
to a clearing where black tumuli rise:
The werelings are fed on blood of their dead
sires as an ancient change seizes hold,
wolf-fire searing the tears from their eyes.

Kiss of Life

Manuel Arenas

As Nótt rides her dusky steed across the Germanic empyrean, bringing night upon a riparian locale in the northern woodland, and wolf-driven Máni speckles the forest canopy in argent refulgence, an eldritch scene is brought to light upon the roof of a dark tower house. A supine beauty, her albescent flesh almost luminescent in the lunar lucency, lays straggled across the rooftop, her luxuriant black mane and velvet dress disappearing into the shadows leaving only the cast of her countenance to glimmer in the gloom like a fallen star. Her crepuscular eyes stare vacantly at her astral brethren, and they return her inert gaze in kind.

Her feint had worked; her foe had been lured into a false sense of security, overstayed his vigil, and she dispatched him with acute enmity leaving nothing fit to return post mortem. Using her late captor's key, she frees herself only to find her egress impeded by the flowing river abutting the tower threshold. Not one to be deterred, she grasps the lintel over the doorway and pulls herself onto the face of the tower with what little strength remaining in her ill-fed frame. Clawing her way to the rooftop surface she collapses, effete and bereft, resigning herself to follow the sylvan night song into oblivion, and await the fateful dawn. Sensing her imminent demise, the woodsy denizens of darkness slither and slog from their bosky bowers to keen for their moribund queen.

Howbeit, emerging from their perch under the eaves of the tower in a flurry of coriaceous wings, an umbra of fantastically large vampire bats scud across the face of the moon, momentarily eclipsing its silvery beams to alight upon the fading femme fatale. One by one they crawl, with wings outstretched, across her marmoreal mien to her pallid face and deliver to the ruddy mouth of their ailing sovereign a rivulet of vivifying blood, restoring the Vampiress to her preternatural fettle. Their errand betimes completed, the sanguinary retinue flaff and flutter off for a hemic nightcap ere repairing to their shuddersome cavern lair to roost and await their proximate summons.

Flushed with an evanescent quickening that gives her pallid cheeks a fleeting roseate hue which flares and falls like the death throes of a Mayfly, Morbidezza exhales a dolent sigh, as a sanguinary tear exudes from her violet oculus. With the spryness of a cat she springs to her unshod feet with renewed élan and divests herself of her gore imbrued velvet vestment afore running toward the edge of the tower rooftop from which she seemingly plummets into darkness . . . only to rise again and hover momentarily; her alabastrine thews gleaming in high relief against the piceous cheek of the tourmaline tower are held aloft by a pair of hellacious bat wings that flail the neighboring trees in the vortex of their wake and whip her sable tresses in a writhing frenzy, causing them to coil and spring like black adders above her spectral brow.

Congregating around the blighted detritus of the tower demesne, the children of the night crow and kvell as their darksome mistress deigns to acknowledge their adulation; her erstwhile violet eyes transmogrified to a candescent glare, beam like balefires in the mirk of the night-veiled forest. Then, with a thresh of her sooty wings she darts above the canopy of her blasted environs and soars into the moonlit firmament, like a fury loosed from hell, with her sundered heart scabbing over with wrath and her morbid mind overbrimming with bloodshed.

The Last Golem

Allan Rozinski

The last golem has been
loosed upon the world,
shaped by the basest impulses of man
into a dreaded, loathsome form;
yet somehow unfinished, incomplete,
with a hunger that knows no end.

Molded from the cursed clay
that feeds the seeds of nightmare blooms,
the poisoned soil that is the mother
to madness.

The last golem's grim purpose
emerges, ruthless in its pursuit
of revenge for both the
bloodthirsty aggressors and
those they have oppressed.

The frenzied friction of battle
throws off countless sparks
into the midst
of humanity's twisted mix
of imagery and desire,
igniting the black heart's kindling,

feeding and fanning the flames
that rise and rage to spread
the ancient sermons
of the inverted gospel.

. . . Now we thrust open the doors of bedlam wide . . .

Make way, make way for the purging fire!
Behold! The other son of man darkly cometh . . .

A Summoning of Demons

Michelle Jeffrey

O fallen angel, O spirit unclean,
However heinous and obscene;
Be thou but the fiercest fiend,
From the very darkness weaned,
Nurtured fast on dread and slaughter,
Thou who dwell across the water,
Beyond the bounds of space and time,
From nether regions' fiery clime,
Come, cross the river of life and death,
With burning eyes and blazing breath!
Come hither now with ravening bent,
In answer to this summons sent!

Beelzebub, thou of envy and spite,
Come storming from the realm of night!
Belphegor, cause thyself to shift,
Come voracious, across the rift!
Asmodeus, thou who stirs the blood,
Licentious, lust and passions flood!
Baal and Hadad, come together,
With thou rain and stormy weather!
Sathanas, wild with wrathful ire,
Come thou from the realms of fire!

Mammon, heavy with rapacious greed,
With appetite strong and avarice freed!
Lucifer, proud with blinding light,
That shines eternal burning bright!

Demons mighty, strong and tall,
Greatest gods before the fall,
Indomitable, rampant, wild and savage,
Unbridled, set to storm and ravage,
Monstrous with malevolent grace,
Hither, come unto this space!

Astral Parasites

Manuel Pérez-Campos

I have attracted, through overindulgence
in paleness, a clique of intervital
psycho freakheads, cowled and enrobed in frail
azure luminescence, who stick round me
and whisper in contrapuntal medley
day and night with necromantic diligence
of potent reasons to self-immolate
and join them beyond the ivory gate
in hell: the way they touch me subtly on
back and shoulder to control me renders
me unequal to the task of brightness
being expected beyond each drawn curtain.
Negatived to the core through their animus
am I, who must soon be blown with them, an
emissary of the stuff of nightmares.

The Silent Silver Sea

Leigh Blackmore

The sea of silent silver lies
Where pockmarked moons ride purple skies.
Here once, my long-lost love with me
Stood, rapturous, near that silver sea.

The silent, silvern sea spreads calm.
I walk its shore 'neath fronded palm,
Remembering my love, how we
Clasped close beside that silent sea.

The soundless, silver sea recedes
Horizonwards, as it proceeds
Upon its way; we were so free
When walking by that soundless sea.

By soundless, silvern sea we loved
And by our vows our love we proved,
So long ago. O, set me free!
Can she yet live near silver sea?

Near silvern, silent sea we pledged
Undying love, near seaside edged
With flotsam, jetsam; so carefree
Were we beside that silent sea.

Homer Before the Trojan Court

Darrell Schweitzer

Did the Trojan ghosts summon
Homer himself to perform before them?
Did Priam, Hecuba, Paris, Hector, Cassandra,
even little Astynax hear him sing
of all they had lost?
Were they moved by the beautiful strains of the *Iliad*
to mourn for the countless, anonymous men
sent into the eternal dark because of
the relentless pride of heroes?
Or did they rage for revenge?
Did they cry out in pity for themselves,
or was that just the wind?
Did Homer, with hearing made more acute by his blindness,
realize that he was among the dead,
and did he, with greatest dignity,
without faltering once,
continue on to the end of the poem?

Was Helen there?
Did *she* weep?

The Witch's Cat

Deborah L. Davitt

She lived alone, as she'd always wished to;
no husband or children to trouble her,
and yet she brewed a broth of bitter rue.

She crafted medicines from balsam fir,
attended births of cows and humans both;
no husband or children to trouble her

meant she had time for such personal growth!
She read both spells and improving books, she
attended births of cows and humans both,

gossiped with neighbors and drank cold mint tea
(secretly admitting she was lonely)—
she read both spells and improving books, she

worked a charm on her cat, Mr. Beastly.
Her cat turned human now, three days a week.
She had admitted that she was lonely—

no more silence now when she wished to speak.
She lived alone, as she'd always wished to,
but her cat turned human three days a week,
and she no longer brewed a broth of bitter rue.

In Arcadia

Josh Maybrook

Beneath the cedarn shadows, solemn fauns,
Reposing, lie serene by hollow caves
And flowered hills and dew-moist river lawns.
In the cool diurnal breeze, the lily waves
Its drowsy bloom, and faerie-things in air
Flit wantonly like playful little knaves.
Enchanted nymphs, unclad with streaming hair,
In idle frolic pass the fleeting hours
Till Twilight's dim and softly-fading glare
Suspires, and they retreat to forest bowers
To dream of joys and pleasures fairer than
Our world's upon their beds of moss and flowers.
Such beauty dwells in the realm of ancient Pan—
Where it is hid, a mystery to man.

My Loveliest Manticore; or, The Queen of the Lamiae

Wade German

Of all my manticores, I love you most. You dissect me with monstrous logic and reassemble my mind anew. But do not tell the others; they love me in their mediocre ways. Perfumed, oiled, and nubile, my ancient flesh awaits! But as you extend and retract your talons back and forth in apparent boredom, on the balcony that overlooks the city of the lamias spread out below the illuminating green field of fungus that grows on the cavernous vault that is our sky, the wisp of an omen, dressed in a bridal gown stolen from the tomb of a desiccated mummy, stands before me, a vision of loveliness streaked through with vibrant pink veins of horror. But you have set aside your golden crown and placed it upon the bedside table, and I am momentarily distracted by the candle flames reflected in the mysterious black orbs that are your eyes. Of all my manticores, I love you most. When I pluck them from their sockets, polish them, then gaze into them for an exquisite duration of divinatory purpose, your pleasurable groans raise the hairs on my shaven head; you tremble with volcanic archipelagoes of ecstasy when I place them, ever so gently, back into the receiving holes! Now take your repast (I see that your ancient appetite, whiter than any old man's beard, extends beyond me). The chamber floor begins to ebb and pulse with oceanic motion, with the torrential volumes of plasma spouting from the unhappy wounds you gouge into my servants. What more to please my prideful king? Do not worry; the dead slaves will soak up their own viscera with the fibrous skeleton of a giant sponge. The omen was a good one; or, if that high promontory amid the ever-shifting planes of perspective which you grope upon has any humour, one of enigma and incorrigible evil . . . Of all my manticores, I love you most!

The Conjuring

Frank Coffman

Often by day, but often by candlelight,
The Conjurer makes ready for the task,
Called by some voice that will not cease to ask,
A Spirit demanding that—through words and sleight
Of mind—a Thing be called forth from oblivion
To find a life among us in this Zone,
To live among us—though not flesh and bone.
The Sage, thus summoned, halts at first—but then:

The chanting inner voice first sinks, then swells;
Thoughts tangle in the mind, wild wordings rage—
Then coalesce, rewarding the conjuring Mage
With a gift most worthy of enduréd hells
And the sweet and bitter draughts from Muse's Wells.
A poem appears most wondrously on a page.

Wildfires

Christina Sng

Wildfires,
Untempered by rain,
Rage through my village,
Leaving most of us dead
Or irreversibly marked,
The ravenous fire burned
In our brains.

Even I,
Swift-footed and fast,
Wear the scars
Like a second skin.
It is never as strong
As the first, permeable,
Vulnerable as echoes.

You,
With your pristine face
And forked tongue,
Charm me for a time
Until the venom you spew
Turns black and green,
Tar-thick and sticky

As is the woman you hide,
Her flesh, mottled glue.

You never told us
You keep them in wax,
All your trophies,
Scattered with lies
To keep them alive.

I discover this too late—
Bearing not one
But two of your babes,
Who unlike you and me,
Are born truly pure,
Their goodness untouched
By your venom and fire.

I paint their backs
With dragon wings,
Nurturing them
Till they are fully grown.
Fierce and unwavering,
Loyal to a fault, they dream
Of changing the world.

First they free me
From my shackles,
Trample the steel cage
I was put in,

Scorching my back
With dragon fire,
Erasing the scars of old.

Reborn,
I sprout wings of my own,
Black and poisoned,
But they fall away like dead skin.
Beneath, my wings are luminous,
Lighting the way forward
In the jet-black night.

I turn back to you,
Engulfing you
And your wax woman
With purifying fire.
You dissolve, cleansed,
Oozing into the earth,
Leaving nothing but dust.

My children and I
Leave this cursed land.
Our wings lift us far beyond
The clouds where we soar,
Unbidden,
Like wildfire,
Untempered by rain.

Now and Forever

Kieran Dacey Boylan

It was written in stone by the gods of the earth
And witnessed by the light of our sun;
All things that have crawled since original birth
Will suffer, and suffer as one.

Ever since I was young have I longed to disown
These words of insidious verse,
But I can't lift the weight of that terrible stone
Where inscribed is humanity's curse.

So with sorrow and anger I burdened the sky,
Imploring the end of all pain.
What I witnessed I never could score from my mind
And hardly can speak of again.

With a passionate fury I openly scorned
All sorrow and madness and fear;
But the howling refrain of existence was gone—
Never again to appear.

Abolished was pain and the source of all pain—
Words unsaid, but I knew it was so.
Then a trembling boom bid a thousand stars rain
From the heavens above to below.

And the infinite span of the gaping black maw
That had spawned each of infinite woes,
Distending its realm of unending abyss,
Yawned wide, then forever did close.

I opened my eyes from that terrible sight
Like an animal gasping for air.
And still to this day am I frozen with fright
When into far places I stare,

For I know there's no temporal end to our pain,
Nor an ultimate evil to sever.
We suffer as one—the alternative is
Oblivion now and forever.

Stela of Selos

Scott J. Couturier

Stela of Selos—
disclose your tale.
Reveal where the eye
of Hirtubor is kept,
where the eels of
Queen Nitrubos
swim in sentry
over sunken titans who
sleep, have slept
since Time's incipience.

Stela of Selos—
divulge the formulae
of Ustar, the runes
of ulterior Alaquay.
Graven by inhuman hand—
scoured by sand
& eternity's grain—
Speak, O stone,
secrets even elder gods
have for black ages forgot!

Stela of Selos—
sacrifice your decipherer.
Blood crusts your
abraded hieroglyphic glaze.

An offering must be made—
flash of knife, mazes
of red curl into contours
of symbology ages-faint.
I see now your meanings!—
illumined by my dying heart's
lurid paint.

Southern Gothic; or, Hillbilly Horror

Carl E. Reed

Of course the corpse were stuffed wit gorse
    it were neither red nor yeller
but mossy green & most obscene;
    Ma hollered at the feller.

The undead gimp had quite a limp,
    the hound chewed off 'is balls;
& now it blunders inter tables,
    chairs, & beds, & walls.

Muh family lost the farm, it's true,
    when Daddy died of cancer;
but glory be! & Lordy, gee!
    Ned turned necromancer

& used 'is cornpone magic
    to raise Daddy from the dead;
muh lil' brother, a-wizardin',
    woke Poppa gimp, but what of Jed?

A-molderin', et up by worms,
    gunned down by the F.B.I.
late last year bootleggin' beer—
    Ma vows: *We'll raise 'im by-&-by,*

though fer now y'all watch Daddy
          to ensure no further harm
come to 'im what love 'is kin.
          Dern! Eee jes' fell & lost 'is arms!

The Egyptian Splendor

Ross Balcom

a creature part human, part lion, part scarab
writhes in my brain

luminous words cavort like jackals
on my tongue

O prophesy—speak for the silent dead,
for the mute and sleeping mummies

jewel-encrusted pyramids are thrust apex-first
into my eyes

my vision bleeds into the Nile almighty,
and crocodiles feed on my screams

O die—nourish the Sun's creatures,
the bloodthirsty children of Light

I copulate with hawk and cat and scorpion
in the erotic desert vastness

I give birth to marvels, mysteries, and miracles—
to the blinding splendor of Now

O rise—inherit the Earth,
the emerald expanse of Forever

Carrion Dreams

Maxwell I. Gold

I found myself wandering in marshes filled with putrid toad shade where, under the black stars, purple winged Näigöths exhaled a rotting delight across my face as they hungered for death. As I waded through the sludge that splattered underneath my steps, thorny weeds covered in birthwort and stinkhorn filled my vision as they and other twisted alien mycotrophic plants contorted around a great tower, stretching lazily toward broken clouds and shattered horizons. Littered with red skunk cabbages at its base, a carrion scent soon made my nose run with blood, as I stumbled over toward its black heart, ignorant of the dark wonders that lay ahead.

The tower—whose skin of obsidian and igneous scales swayed like a lowly beacon in the middle of a forest wrought by the overwhelming scent of death, amidst an endless droning that rained down from the sky in the form of flies, locusts, and acidic rain—filled me a familiarity that I could not discern. It was like some dream or wild vision. The otherwise wretched smog created a mystifying blanket as I climbed the spiral stairs lining the labyrinthine rim of the tower. Finally, atop the obelisk of marble and bone, I wandered into a dreamy mausolean temple, where shadows and time pulled me closer to some awful truth. The winged beasts again howled, their mouths yawning toward the vast spectral majesty above dripping with ancient lust. Beyond the doors of this shrine, their cries worsened as I wandered inside, as if some awful deed had been committed, something that could never be unseen. The scent of decay became worse, thicker like a viscous fluid that flooded my lungs making breathing nearly impossible.

Soon the lights had all gone dark and the flames withered into ash, filling my soul with a menacing feeling as if I'd been here before. The world I found myself in, these creatures moaning in a raucous symphony, were like a nightmarish memory my mind desperately wished to suppress. My body shuddered as I approached a slab in the vaulted room, where clawed hooves clamored above at an opening like vultures; their mouths waiting, dripping and glaring down eagerly at the body below them. Seemingly ignoring me, only wishing to feed on the carcass.

In that awful moment, I knew not to look at the face on the slab, for I knew that it would be more familiar to me in its alabaster repose than the bones beneath the scalding flesh of my own worn visage. The weight of that ghastly truth held such a revelation that I would have rather been crushed by the immensities of my own vast ignorance and naïveté, while secretly letting the deadly realization fester and burrow deeper into my heart. This was the garden of my nightmares, a ghoulish plot littered with the seeds of my soul and I was forever its caretaker.

Classic Reprints

In a Breton Cemetery

Ernest Dowson

They sleep well here,
    These fisher-folk who passed their anxious days
    In fierce Atlantic ways;
And found not there,
    Beneath the long curled wave,
    So quiet a grave.

And they sleep well
    These peasant-folk, who told their lives away,
    From day to market-day,
As one should tell,
    With patient industry,
    Some sad old rosary.

And now night falls,
    Me, tempest-tost, and driven from pillar to post,
    A poor worn ghost,
This quiet pasture calls;
    And dear dead people with pale hands
    Beckon me to their lands.

[First published in the *Pageant* (1897).]

The Vampire

Arthur Symons

Intolerable woman, where's the name
For your insane complexity of shame?
Vampire! white bloodless creature of the night,
Whose lust of blood has blanched her chill veins white,
Veins fed with moonlight over dead men's tombs;
Whose eyes remember many martyrdoms,
So that their depths, whose depth cannot be found,
Are shadowed pools in which a soul lies drowned;
Who would fain have pity, but she may not rest
Till she have sucked a man's heart from his breast,
And drained his life-blood from him, vein by vein,
And seen his eyes grow brighter for the pain,
And his lips sigh her name with his last breath,
As the man swoons ecstatically on death.

[Reprinted from Symons's *Lesbia and Other Poems* (New York: E. P. Dutton, 1920).]

Reviews

A Golgotha of Horror

S. T. Joshi

WADE GERMAN. *The Ladies of the Everlasting Lichen and Other Relics.*
Bucharest, Romania: Mount Abraxas Press, 2019. 72 pp. 75 euros hc.
Limited to 88 copies.

The Canadian poet Wade German has definitively established himself as
one of the premier weird poets of our time, joining Ann K. Schwader,
Kyla Lee Ward, and a few others in that lofty rank. And yet, until the
appearance of this latest volume, he had published only a single
collection of poems, *Dreams from a Black Nebula* (Hippocampus Press,
2014). This new book, relatively slim as it is, goes far in confirming
German's high standing as a poet, and it is a shame that the book's
minuscule print run and high price might severely limit its readership.

German's poetry is characterized by meticulous attention to the
formal meters he employs (most notably the sonnet, but also the
quatrain and other stanzaic forms, the triolet, and even the compressed
verse drama, of which we have several shining examples in the present
book). He can evoke terror with a single line or even a single word; and
yet, his poems are far from mere shudder-coining, becoming thought-
provoking meditations on the fragility of our tenure on this pain-
wracked globe.

Poets do not need to establish any kind of overriding theme or motif
in a collection, but I detect two such motifs in this book. The first is
religion—or, perhaps more accurately, the perversion of religion, or the
establishment of a dark religion of death, decay, and terror as a grim
parody of the conventional religions of the earth, which seek to provide

an antidote (spurious, in my mind) to the "thousand natural shocks that flesh is heir to."

One of the most evocative of German's poems in this book is "Ride of the Witchfinder," a magnificent sonnet on the eternal punishment meted out to a persecutor of witches. It deserves quotation in full:

> I slew them all, and watched their corpses burn
> In flames that rose by forces not my own,
> Then witnessed all their evil ashes blown
> By winds that voiced the vows of their return.
> And as I rode, the very sky went black,
> Subverting day to never-ending night
> As nails of horror hammered in my sight—
> Black magic vengeance followed in my tracks.
>
> And so I ride as one who flees from sin,
> Pursued by shadow-things that curse and scream
> Across a world become a dead god's dream,
> Abominated, bare, my soul worn thin—
> Three hundred years, and on and on I ride
> Through endless hells—and Hell's no place to hide.

Other poems elaborate upon the (anti-)religious theme. I cannot tell if "Out of Endor" has any specific connection with the Old Testament account of the Witch of Endor, who summoned up the shade of Samuel; but the baleful first stanza of the poem is memorable:

> The horned red moon has risen clear,
> And evening augurs heresies;
> The rites and rituals commence—
> And demon principalities
> Grow silent momently to hear
> Our song of strange malevolence.

"Ecclesiastical Triptych" is more forthright subversion of Christian myth, and its third section provides the title for the book; that section's repeated use of "lichen" in multiple different contexts provides a haunting ritornello to a memorable poetic sequence. Also explicitly biblical is "Methusaleh"; but here, that ancient figure's nine hundred-odd years on this planet have turned him into a misanthrope who loathes the moral and physical corruption of the human race.

The second major motif in this book is German's skillful riffs on the long history of weird fiction and poetry. "The Driver of the Dragon's Coach" is set in the realm of Stoker's *Dracula*; "The Secret Prayer of Victor Frankenstein" betrays its source in its very title; "Naotalba's Song" purports to be a segment from the play *The King in Yellow*. More significantly, "Lore" is a 100-line poem that elaborates upon Lovecraft's theme of the forbidden book, and its concluding lines effectively convey Lovecraft's cosmicism:

> An apostate, I keep the eldritch lore,
> The revelation of an elder faith—
> Our world is but an altar in the void
> Where souls shall be devoured and destroyed.

"Beddoes: Marginalia in a Cadaveric Atlas" is presumably an expansion of Thomas Lovell Beddoes's *Death's Jest-Book* (1850), taking the form of a short verse drama. "The Ghosts of Hyperborea" is a nod to Clark Ashton Smith. And we can hardly bypass "The Tomb of Wilum Hopfrog Pugmire," a moving elegy that seeks to capture the essence of that late author's imaginative realm.

Other poems in the book do not fit easily into the two rubrics outlined above, but they are no less vital and dynamic. "Wraiths" features a memorable passage where metaphor is used to telling effect: "We are as exiles who exist / Like lovers long-since left behind / In mausoleums of your mind . . ."

The book concludes with three long poems featuring figures from Greek myth. Historically, weird poets have not drawn frequently on this body of myth, since its major features appear to convey an atmosphere of light-hearted paganism; but there are plenty of dark corners in Greek myth that a poet of German's skill can exploit.

"Scylla and Charybdis" is a meditation on those two baleful creatures whom Odysseus encountered in his voyages, as recounted in Homer's *Odyssey*. The eponymous figure of the poem "Eurynomos" is much more obscure, and German helpfully provides an epigraph from

Pausanias, who writes that Eurynomos is "one of the spirits of the Underworld, who devours the flesh of corpses, leaving only bones." This sounds highly promising; and German's poem insidiously morphs from a catalogue of body horror and decay to a chilling indictment of human frailty, moral and physical. The book concludes with "Gorgonum Chaos," a poetic dialogue between Stheno and Euryale, the sisters of Medusa, who lament the demise of their sibling at the hands of Perseus and curse the goddess Athena for encouraging that valiant hero.

The production of this book calls for especial praise. The typeface is suitably archaic, the paper stiff and heavy, and scattered throughout the book are peculiar illustrations taken from what I take to be an 1825 book on black and white magic. This is a book to savor in small doses; each poem is evocative and striking in its own way, and the lengthier poems are Golgothas of horror and grue that will long linger in the mind. It can only be hoped that the poems in the book will one day reach a wider audience.

Dark Oracles Indeed

Donald Sidney-Fryer

D. L. MYERS. *Oracles from the Black Pool.* New York: Hippocampus Press, 2019. 136 pp. Cover art and 21 illustrations by Daniel V. Sauer. $15.00 tpb.

This is a magnificent little volume remarkable not only for its contents—its raison d'être, the original poetry—but for the striking and original art as manifested on its front cover, no less than the nearly two dozen illustrations inside the book. Even if only a slender volume at 136 pages, it packs a wallop with its substantial main text. Myers here presents himself (thanks to Derrick Hussey's ongoing crusade on behalf of new poetry through Hippocampus Press) as an exceptional poet, strong and intense, even if cloaked outwardly as a calm and moderate-seeming individual in the everyday social milieu. The book itself arrives very well recommended and judiciously so, preceded by a notable preface of appreciation by K. A. Opperman, and succeeded after the main text by four deserved tributes from his siblinghood of poet-friends, Opperman, Ashley Dioses, and the irrepressible balladeer par excellence, Adam Bolivar. We had thought that dark fantasy as expressed in verse had exhausted itself, but no, this magisterial small volume proves the present critic wrong. The three poets along with Myers himself make up a special cénacle (connected in person or electronically by the Internet) that calls itself the Crimson Circle; the crimson requires no gloss.

Myers is a strong and inventive traditionalist, working within older forms, meters, and rime, and performing very well, no less than in free verse and prose-poetry. Whether experienced as presented here front to back, or merely sampled casually here and there, these poems, these oracles, prove a constant revelation, especially as punctuated by small pieces of verse, such as these four haiku, which we quote as our first citations, as evidence of Myers's invention and imagination.

Haiku One

Longing for snowflakes
In hot California sun
Tree waits for kisses.

Haiku Two

Undulating leaf
Restlessly waiting for wind
To take flight again.

Haiku Three

Ice-cold, grey rain clouds
Lie broken a cross blue sky
While I sit gazing.

Haiku Four

Her profile flutters
Among stray strands of brown flax
Tempest waves as silk.

Myers has created an exceptional ambiance for his macabre visions, a new town creatively and beautifully called Yorehaven (a memorable name), to be found somewhere not far away from Lovecraft's Arkham or Innsmouth or his own Providence, Rhode Island, as reimagined by that master in his darkling fictions major or minor, in verse and in prose. We might personally hesitate to visit Yorehaven ourselves unless escorted by a goodly company of sibling aficionados possibly armed with clubs, spears, guns, and pistols. The ambiance to which Myers introduces us appears to teem with a variety of monsters including vampires, werewolves, and more intimidating prodigies of terror or even horror as spawned from the author's ever prodigal imagination—eek! (Let us hide under the covers or under the bed.) Never mind bizarre specimens from the plant kingdom!

The Phosphorescent Fungi

A crawling darkness pressed upon my eyes
In which a moiling sea of phantoms swam,
And crazed, I hungered for a numbing dram
To send my mind to where all reason flies,
Until before me rose a fitful fire,
A corpse-light foul and bruised that chilled my soul,

Yet drew me onward toward a ghastly goal—
A grotto burning like a purple pyre!

And then I saw the things that cast that glow,
Pale fungi vile and stained with rank decay ;
And bathed in icy sweat from head to toe,
I stood and quaked before that dire display.
Then evil whispers hissed about my ears,
And I broke down in horror wracked with tears.

Well, we ourselves as reader-critic might very well follow suit! We cannot resist quoting another poem, a succinct quatrain.

Autumn Moon

The gibbous moon in ruddy cowl
Rides wild in the autumnal sky
While coyotes in the cornstalks howl
And dance to see it soaring high.

But these few poems as quoted in this review can give only a tithe of the wealth of grim imagination and invention on display in this volume, not to leave unmentioned the poet's exquisite craftsmanship. The poet has arranged the more than five dozen morceaux that he presents here as follows, that is, under these inviting seven section titles: The Streets of Yorehaven, The Acolytes of Samhain, The Summons, The Star's Prisoner, The Canker Within, The Temple of the River Goddess, and O Dark Muse. The section of four tributes by his fellow poets comes at the very end of the miniature tome.

Myers find himself in excellent company, in the fine and sympathetic siblinghood of like-minded poet-bards known as the Crimson Circle. He well deserves the tributes, as well as the just and judicious recommendation (on the volume's back cover) as penned by S. T. Joshi, that doyen of connoisseur-critics and creative scholars. Warmest congratulations to poet D. L. Myers first and foremost, next artist D. V. Sauer, and then D. Hussey, Hippocampus Press personified!

Notes on Contributors

By day, **Mike Allen** writes the arts column for the *Roanoke* (VA) *Times*. By night he spins dark fables. An author, editor, and publisher, he has been a finalist for the Nebula, Shirley Jackson, and World Fantasy Awards, as well as a three-time winner of the Rhysling Award for poetry.

Manuel Arenas currently resides in Phoenix, Arizona, where he writes his Gothic fantasies and dark ditties sheltered behind heavy curtains, as he shuns the oppressive orb that glares down on him from the cloudless, dust filled desert sky. His work has appeared in various genre publications, most notably in *Spectral Realms*.

Chelsea Arrington has a predilection for things dark and romantic. Among her favorite authors are Algernon Charles Swinburne, Lord Dunsany, and Ray Bradbury. She likes her steaks rare and her wine as dry as graveyard dirt. Her poetry has appeared in the anthology *Folk Horror Revival: Corpse Roads*, *Spectral Realms*, and *Audient Void*. She lives in Southern California with her boyfriend, her nephew, and two lap dogs.

Ross Balcom lives in Southern California. His poems have appeared in *Beyond Centauri*, *inkscrawl*, *Poetry Midwest*, *Scifaikuest*, *Star*Line*, and other publications. He is a frequent contributor to *Songs of Eretz Poetry Review*.

David Barker's latest books are *Witches in Dreamland*, a Lovecraftian novel written in collaboration with W. H. Pugmire, from Hippocampus Press, and *Half in Light, Half in Shadow*, a chapbook of weird short stories from Audient Void Publishing.

Leigh Blackmore has written weird verse since age thirteen. He has lived in the Illawarra, New South Wales, Australia, for the last decade. He has edited *Terror Australis: Best Australian Horror* (1993) and *Midnight Echo 5* (2011) and written *Spores from Sharnoth & Other Madnesses* (2008). A nominee for SFPA's Rhysling Award (Best Long Poem), Leigh is also a four-time Ditmar Award nominee. He is currently assembling an edition of *The Selected Letters of Robert Bloch*.

Benjamin Blake was born in 1985 and grew up in the small town of Eltham, New Zealand. He is the author of the novel *The Devil's Children* and the poetry collections *Southpaw Nights, Standing on the Threshold of Madness, Dime Store Poetry,* and the forthcoming *Tenebrae in Aeternum,* to be published by Hippocampus Press.

Adam Bolivar, a native of Boston now residing in Portland, Oregon, has published his weird fiction and poetry in the pages of *Nameless,* the *Lovecraft eZine, Spectral Realms,* and Chaosium's *Steampunk Cthulhu* and *Atomic Age Cthulhu* anthologies. His latest collection, *The Lay of Old Hex,* was published in 2017 by Hippocampus Press.

Frank Coffman is a retired professor of college English and creative writing. He has published speculative poetry, fiction, and scholarly essays in a variety of magazines and anthologies. His poetic magnum opus, *The Coven's Hornbook and Other Poems* (January 2019), has been followed by his rendition into English verse of 327 quatrains in his collection *Khayyám's Rubáiyát* (May 2019). Both books were published by Bold Venture Press.

Scott J. Couturier is a writer of the weird, grotesque, perverse, and darkly fantastic. His prose and poetry have appeared in numerous venues, including *Audient Void, Spectral Realms, Hinnom Magazine, Eternal Haunted Summer, Weirdbook,* and the *Test Patterns & Pulps* series of anthologies from Planet X Publications. He lives an elusive reverie in the wilds of Northern Michigan.

Nicole Cushing is the Bram Stoker Award–winning author of *Mr. Suicide* and two-time nominee for the Shirley Jackson Award. Her second novel, *A Sick Gray Laugh,* was recently released by Word Horde. A stand-alone novella, *The Half-Freaks* (published by Grimscribe Press), also appeared in 2019. Nicole lives and works in Indiana.

Deborah L. Davitt was raised in Nevada but currently lives in Houston, Texas with her husband and son. Her poetry has received Rhysling, Dwarf Star, and Pushcart nominations; her short fiction has appeared in *Galaxy's Edge, Intergalactic Medicine*

Show, and Pseudopod. For more about her work, including her Edda-Earth novels and her poetry collection, *The Gates of Never.*

Holly Day's poetry has recently appeared in *Asimov's Science Fiction, Grain,* and the *Tampa review.* Her newest poetry collections are *In This Place, She Is Her Own, A Wall to Protect Your Eyes, Where We Went Wrong,* and *Cross Referencing a Book of Summer,* while her newest nonfiction books are *Music Theory for Dummies* and *Tattoo FAQ.*

Ashley Dioses is a writer of dark poetry and fiction from southern California. Her debut collection of dark traditional poetry, *Diary of a Sorceress,* was released in 2017 from Hippocampus Press. Her second poetry collection of early works, *The Withering,* is forthcoming from Gehenna and Hinnom Books this autumn.

Cataloging librarian **Adele Gardner** is an active member of HWA with a master's in English literature. She has published a poetry book (*Dreaming of Days in Astophel*) and more than 400 poems, stories, art, and essays in Flame Tree's *Lost Souls* and *Haunted House* anthologies, *Strange Horizons, NewMyths.com, Mythic Delirium, Horror Garage* (Paula Guran), and more. She recently curated the SFPA 2019 Halloween Poetry Reading.

Wade German is the author of two collections of poetry, *The Ladies of the Everlasting Lichen and Other Relics* (Mount Abraxas Press, 2019) and *Dreams from a Black Nebula* (Hippocampus Press, 2014). His poems have been nominated for the Rhysling, Elgin, and Pushcart awards, and have received numerous honorable mentions in Ellen Datlow's *Best Horror of the Year* anthologies. His work has appeared most recently in *Spectral Realms, Weird Fiction Review, The Averoigne Legacy* (Pickman's Press, 2019), and *Best of Black Wings* (PS Publishing, 2019).

Maxwell I. Gold is an author of weird fiction and dark fantasy. His work has been published in *Spectral Realms, Audient Void, Hinnom Magazine,* and elsewhere. His short story "A Credible Fear" will be published in the literary journal *The Offbeat* from Michigan State University's Department of Creative Writing and Rhetoric. He studied philosophy and political science at the University of Toledo and is an active member of the Horror Writers Association.

Chad Hensley is a poet and author. His first book of poetry, *Embrace the Hideous Immaculate*, was published in May 2014 from Raw Dog Screaming Press. His recent poetry appearances include the *Horror Writers Association Horror Poetry Showcase III, Weirdbook,* and the first four issues of *Spectral Realms.* Look for a new version of his nonfiction book *EsoTerra: The Journal of Extreme Culture* later this year.

Cecelia Hopkins-Drewer lives in Adelaide, South Australia. She has had science fiction poetry published in the *Mentor,* a fanzine edited by Ron Clarke, and participates in an online poetry community known as "Poetry Soup." She also has flash fiction pieces in an anthology entitled *Worlds: Dark Drabbles #1,* edited by Dean Kershaw, and articles in the *Lovecraft Annual.* (She has also been known by her maiden name "Hopkins" and her married name "Drewer.")

Michelle Jeffrey has been writing poetry, prose, and short stories from a very young age. She is a regular contributor to pagan magazines in Australia. Her mother introduced her to horror movies and read horror stories to her as a young girl, sparking off a lifelong love of the horror genre.

S. T. Joshi is a widely published critic and editor. He has prepared editions of the collected poetry of H. P. Lovecraft, Clark Ashton Smith, Donald Wandrei, George Sterling, and H. L. Mencken. He is the editor of *Spectral Realms.*

Curtis M. Lawson is the author of unapologetically weird and transgressive fiction, dark poetry, and graphic novels. His work ranges from technicolor pulp adventures to bleak cosmic horror and includes *The Devoured, It's a Bad, Bad, Bad, Bad World,* and *Black Heart Boys' Choir.* He is a member of the Horror Writers Association and the organizer of the *Weird Live Horror* reading series. He lives in Salem, Mass., with his wife and their son.

Mack W. Mani is an award-winning screenwriter, poet, and author. His work has appeared in *Strange Horizons, NewMyths,* and the *Pedestal Magazine.* In 2018 he won Best Screenplay at the H. P. Lovecraft Film Festival. He currently lives in Portland, Oregon.

Josh Maybrook is an American poet living in Edinburgh, Scotland. His poems, written largely in traditional verse forms, draw influence from weird fiction, classical mythology, and long walks in rural landscapes.

Michael D. Miller is an adjunct professor and NEH medievalist summer scholar and authored the *Realms of Fantasy RPG* for Mythopoeia Games Publications. His poetry has appeared *Spectral Realms*, scholarly articles in *Lovecraft Annual*, reviews in *Dead Reckonings* and *Dim Shores*, and essays in *Crackpot Press* and *Marchxness*.

K. A. Opperman is a poet with a predilection for the strange, the Gothic, and the grotesque, continuing the macabre and fantastical tradition of such luminaries as Poe, Clark Ashton Smith, and H. P. Lovecraft. His first verse collection, *The Crimson Tome*, was published by Hippocampus Press in 2015.

Manuel Pérez-Campos's poetry has appeared previously in *Spectral Realms* and *Weird Fiction Review*. A collection of his poetry in the key of the weird is in progress; so is a collection of ground-breaking essays on H. P. Lovecraft. He lives in Bayamón, Puerto Rico.

Carl E. Reed is currently employed as the showroom manager for a window, siding, and door company just outside Chicago. Former jobs include U.S. marine, long-haul trucker, improvisational actor, cab driver, security guard, bus driver, door-to-door encyclopedia salesman, construction worker, and art show MC. His poetry has been published in the *Iconoclast* and *Spectral Realms*; short stories in *Black Gate* and *newWitch* magazines.

Allan Rozinski is a writer of speculative fiction and poetry who has most recently had poetry either accepted or published in *HWA Poetry Showcase Volume V*, *Spectral Realms*, *Outposts of Beyond*, *Star*Line*, and *Weirdbook*. He can be found on Facebook and Twitter.

David Sammons lives in South Yorkshire, UK. A devotee of weird fiction, he is currently reading through the large number of books mentioned in Lovecraft's "Supernatural Horror in Literature." This interest in weird literature has gradually developed into a desire to create his own. He has written a small amount of short fiction and some poems. This is the first piece to be published.

Darrell Schweitzer is a short story writer and novelist, and former coeditor of *Weird Tales.* He has published much humorous Lovecraftian verse (*Non Compost Mentis* [Zadok Allen, 1993] et al.) and also has two serious poetry collections in print, *Groping toward the Light* (Wildside Press, 2000) and *Ghosts of Past and Future* (Wildside Press, 2008).

Donald Sidney-Fryer is the author of *Emperor of Dreams: A Clark Ashton Smith Bibliography* (Donald M. Grant, 1978), *The Atlantis Fragments* (Hippocampus Press, 2009), and many other volumes. He has edited Smith's *Poems in Prose* (Arkham House, 1965) and written many books and articles on California poets. His autobiography *Hobgoblin Apollo* (2016) and two volumes of miscellany, *Aesthetics Ho!* (2017) and *West of Wherevermore* (2019), have been published by Hippocampus Press.

Christina Sng is the Bram Stoker Award–winning author of *A Collection of Nightmares* (Raw Dog Screaming Press, 2017). Her poetry has appeared in numerous venues worldwide, including *Apex Magazine, Cricket, New Myths, Polu Texni,* and *Space and Time,* and received nominations in the Rhysling Awards, the Dwarf Stars, the Elgin Awards, and honorable mentions in *The Year's Best Fantasy and Horror* and *The Best Horror of the Year.*

Thomas Tyrrell lives in Birmingham, UK, where the Gothic is more Post-Industrial and less Southern. His short story "The Coronation Service" is published in *Hellfire Crossroads 7,* now available in paperback and Kindle, and his piratical poetry pamphlet, *The Poor Rogues Hang,* will be published by Mosaique Press in 2020. He has a Ph.D in English Literature from Cardiff University.

Don Webb, who has been nominated for the Rhysling Award and the International Horror Critics Award, is the principal of the women's high school in the Lockhart Work Project. He has a new full-length poetry collection, *From Deep Dendo* (Dunhams Manor Press). He teaches horror writing for UCLA Extension.

M. F. Webb's poetry has appeared in previous issues of *Spectral Realms* and her fiction has been published in *Latchkey Tales*. She resides in a Victorian seaport town not too far from Seattle with her husband and their five cats.

Mary Krawczak Wilson has written poetry, fiction, plays, articles, and essays. She was born in St. Paul, Minnesota, and moved to Seattle in 1991. Her most recent essay appeared in the *American Rationalist*.

CPSIA information can be obtained
at www.ICGtesting.com
Printed in the USA
BVHW072041130223
658298BV00013B/1916